Bears

Edited by Katie Gillespie

LIGHTB◆X
openlightbox.com

LIGHTBOX

Go to
www.openlightbox.com,
and enter this book's
unique code.

ACCESS CODE

L B B 8 4 6 4 7

Lightbox is an all-inclusive digital solution for the teaching and learning of curriculum topics in an original, groundbreaking way. Lightbox is based on National Curriculum Standards.

STANDARD FEATURES OF LIGHTBOX

AUDIO High-quality narration using text-to-speech system

ACTIVITIES Printable PDFs that can be emailed and graded

SLIDESHOWS Pictorial overviews of key concepts

VIDEOS Embedded high-definition video clips

WEBLINKS Curated links to external, child-safe resources

TRANSPARENCIES Step-by-step layering of maps, diagrams, charts, and timelines

INTERACTIVE MAPS Interactive maps and aerial satellite imagery

QUIZZES Ten multiple choice questions that are automatically graded and emailed for teacher assessment

KEY WORDS Matching key concepts to their definitions

Contents

Meet the Bear

Bears are a type of **mammal**. They usually live by themselves and spend most of their time looking for food. Bears eat plants, such as grasses and berries. They also eat fish, insects, and small animals.

Most bears are large animals with thick fur, round heads, and short tails. Their colors and sizes are different depending on the type of bear. Bears are known for their excellent sense of smell. They can be found in North America, South America, Europe, and Asia. Most bears live in forests and caves.

Bears that live in parts of the world that have a winter season go into **hibernation**. When the weather gets cold, bears cuddle up in a cave or hollowed out tree for months, until spring comes. This way, they can stay warm and avoid the months when food is hard to find.

Bears are one of the few animals that can stand up or walk on two feet.

All about Bears

There are many different types of bears, but only three **species** live in North America. These are brown bears, black bears, and polar bears. Black bears are the smallest, and most common, of the three species.

Polar bears live in the far north, where it is cold. Black bears are located in Canada, and in most U.S. states. Brown bears live in Canada, Alaska, and four other states in the western half of the United States. These include Washington, Idaho, Montana, and Wyoming.

Bear Skull

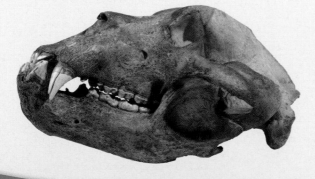

Washington

Oregon

Idaho

Nevada

Utah

California

Arizona

PACIFIC OCEAN

■ Bear Habitat

1 Grizzly & Wolf Discovery Center

2 Vince Shute Wildlife Sanctuary

3 Katmai National Park and Preserve

0   500 Miles

0   500 KM

Bears in America

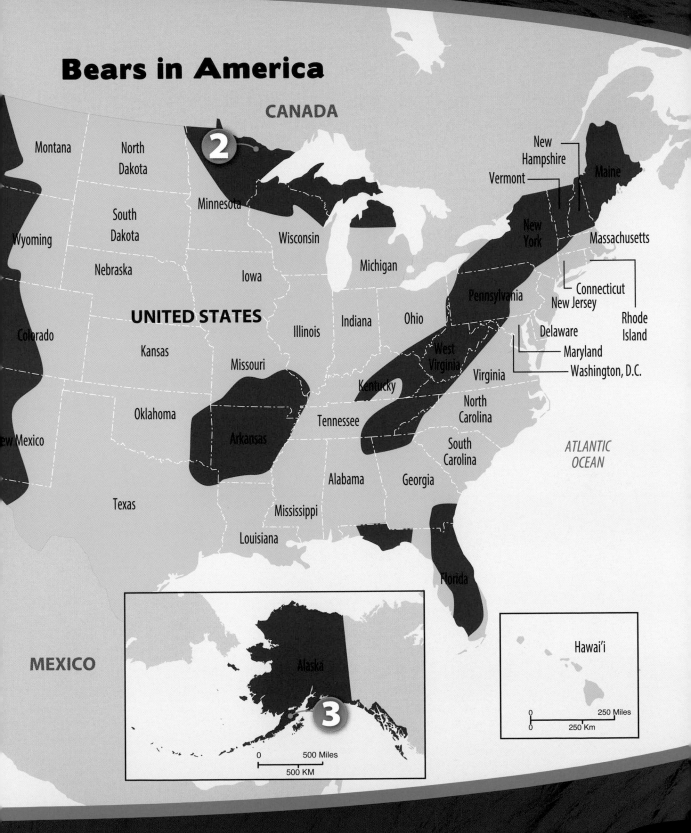

CANADA

Montana

North Dakota

South Dakota

Wyoming

Nebraska

Minnesota

Wisconsin

Michigan

Iowa

UNITED STATES

Colorado

Kansas

Missouri

Illinois

Indiana

Ohio

New York

Pennsylvania

New Hampshire

Vermont

Maine

Massachusetts

Connecticut

New Jersey

Rhode Island

Delaware

Maryland

Washington, D.C.

West Virginia

Virginia

Oklahoma

Arkansas

Tennessee

Kentucky

New Mexico

North Carolina

South Carolina

Texas

Mississippi

Alabama

Georgia

ATLANTIC OCEAN

Louisiana

Florida

MEXICO

Alaska

0   500 Miles

500 KM

Hawai'i

0   250 Miles

0   250 Km

Bear History

Bears come from an ancient animal called the *miacid*. This animal was small in size, had a snout, and lived 50 million years ago. Wolves, hyenas, and weasels also come from miacids.

About 38 million years ago, bearlike animals started to develop the features of bears today. They began to grow larger than other miacids, and their skulls became rounder. Ten million years ago, animals called *ursids* developed. Over time, they became the bears that are common today.

Early ursids, such as the true cave bear, would compete with humans for habitat and food.

Bear Timeline

40 Million Years Ago

The first miacids appear on Earth.

36 Million Years Ago

Ancient **carnivorous** creatures split into two main families, called procyonidae and ursidae.

24 Million Years Ago

The ursidae family begins to **diversify**. The giant panda and the spectacled bear become two different species.

15,000 Years Ago

Bears live all across North America.

1800 to 1975

Between 1800 and 1975, the grizzly bear population in the United States decreases from 100,000 to 1,000.

1900s

Black bear populations drop to dangerously low levels in parts of North America, due to over-hunting. Hunting regulations are put in place to help save the black bear.

Today

Black bear populations are recovering, growing at a rate of 2 percent per year.

Bear Habitat

Bears can live in almost all environments. Some live in dense forests, while others live in cold, icy places. Most bears prefer to live away from humans. Some bears, such as the grizzly, live near campsites, where they hope to find leftover food.

Bears often live in forests that have water close by. Many bears live in **dens**. Dens can be inside caves or the hollow of a tree. Some bears can spend almost half of their lives in dens. They make their dens with old leaves and plants.

Bears have **4 thick paws** with **5 claws** on each paw.

Polar bears can weigh more than **1,700 pounds.** (771 kilograms)

Polar bears can swim **4 to 6 miles per hour**. (6.4 to 9.7 kilometers)

Bears can gain **2.2 pounds** each day to prepare for winter. (1 kg)

Bears rarely use the same den two winters in a row.

Bear Features

Bears have many features that help them survive in nature. A bear's ability to gain a lot of fat on their large, stocky bodies helps them live through harsh winters. They also have powerful muscles. A bear is strong enough to fight off almost any other animal.

FUR
Bears have thick fur that helps them keep warm. The fur covers their entire body.

LEGS
Bears can stand on their hind legs to reach food or to scare off **predators**.

CLAWS
All bears have sharp claws that help them dig and rip through plants and trees. This is useful when bears need to turn, lift, or pull up objects to find food.

HEAD

Bears have large, round skulls. They are smart animals, with a fairly large brain.

NOSE

Most bears have an excellent sense of smell. This helps them find food easily. They use their nose to sniff out plants or animals that are nearby.

TEETH

Bears have strong teeth, with long **canines** to help them eat meat. The teeth are able to tear into tough meat easily.

A brown bear can eat
30 fish per day.

What Do Bears Eat?

Bears are **omnivores**. This means that they eat both meat and plants. However, some types of bears have different diets. This diet depends on where the bear lives. If there are more plants in the bear's habitat, the bear is likely to eat less meat. The giant panda bear is a **herbivore**. Most of its diet is made up of bamboo.

If a bear lives where there is very little plant life, it will eat more meat. The polar bear is a carnivore. It eats mostly meat. Grizzly bears and black bears eat fish as a part of their diet. They have also been known to hunt large animals, such as elk and bison.

The spectacled bear climbs trees to find food.

Bear Life Cycle

The life cycle of a bear depends on the type of bear. Grizzly bears mate between May and July. The male stays with the female for about one month. The female digs a den where she can hibernate for the winter.

Birth

A grizzly bear can have one to four cubs at a time. At birth, grizzly bear cubs cannot open their eyes. The cubs are covered with very tiny hairs and have no teeth. At this stage, the cubs are helpless. Their mothers must care for them.

Early Months

The first few months of a cub's life are spent inside the den with its mother. The cub's eyes open after its first two or three weeks. The cub also starts to grow more hair. The mother bear feeds the cub her milk, which is full of fat and **protein**.

Adults

Adult grizzly bears are very heavy. They can weigh between 700 and 1,700 pounds (317.5 and 771 kg). Males weigh more than females.

First Year

As the weather outside gets warmer, the bears start to explore outside of the den. After six months, they can leave the den with their mother. At this stage, the cubs grow very fast. They learn skills, such as hunting, by watching their mother.

Encountering Bears

Bears can be found in nature and in zoos. Some bears live in areas where there are more humans. For instance, bears can be found near campgrounds in the woods.

Humans sometimes leave leftover food at campsites. Bears may come to the sites searching for food. It is very important to clean up campsites and to not leave food out. Garbage should be thrown away in locking, bear-proof garbage bins.

If a bear does show up in a campsite, it should not be approached. It is best to remain calm and leave the area slowly. Never go near a bear cub. A mother bear can be very dangerous if she thinks her young is being threatened.

Bears have **two layers** of fur.

Bears have a better sense of **smell** than a **hound**.

While hibernating, a grizzly bear's **heart rate** slows to eight beats per minute.

 The popular childhood toy **"teddy bear"** was named after **President Teddy Roosevelt.**

Eating human food can make bears sick.

Myths and Legends

There have been many stories about bears from all over the world. The ancient Greeks have a story about how the god Zeus turned a mother and son into bears and then placed them in the sky. Now, they appear as groups of stars known as Great Bear and Little Bear.

American Indians also have many legends about bears. In these legends, bears are often symbols of wisdom and strength. Some stories talk about bears that help heal sick people.

The Big Dipper is a constellation that is part of the larger Great Bear. The bear's tail makes up the dipper's handle.

The Cherokee Bear Legend

The Ani-Tsa-gu-hi Cherokee lived near a forest. They worked very hard to find food. One family had a son who would spend all day in the forest. His parents worried about him. They asked him why he kept going into the forest. He told them that the forest was filled with food and life was easier there. The boy asked his family to come with him.

The boy's parents told the Ani-Tsa-gu-hi leaders the boy's story. After hearing it, they all decided to follow the boy into the forest. Other groups rushed to convince them to change their minds, but the Ani-Tsa-gu-hi told the others that they had changed their name to the *Yonva*, which means "bears." The Yonva then went into the forest. As the other groups walked away, they looked back and saw a group of bears.

Bear Quiz

1 What type of animal is a bear?

2 Where should people throw away garbage while camping?

3 What other constellation is part of Big Bear?

4 On what continents do bears live?

5 During which season do bears hibernate?

6 What is the smallest species of bear in North America?

7 What is the Ani-Tsa-gu-hi word for "bear"?

8 Where does a bear live and sleep?

9 How many cubs can a grizzly bear have at a time?

10 From which ancient animal is the modern bear descended?

Answers: 1. Mammal 2. Locking, bear-proof garbage bins 3. The Big Dipper 4. North America, South America, Europe, and Asia 5. Winter 6. Black bear 7. Yonva 8. In a den 9. One to four 10. The miacid

Key Words

canines: sharp pointy teeth on either side of the mouth

carnivorous: feeding on other animals

dens: places where animals live in nature

diversify: to develop different types of animals within one group

herbivore: an animal that eats plants

hibernation: a period during which an animal remains inactive

mammal: a warm-blooded animal that has a backbone and drinks milk from its mother

predators: animals that hunt other animals for food

protein: a substance found in all living things

species: a group of animals or plants that have many features in common

Index

SUPPLEMENTARY RESOURCES

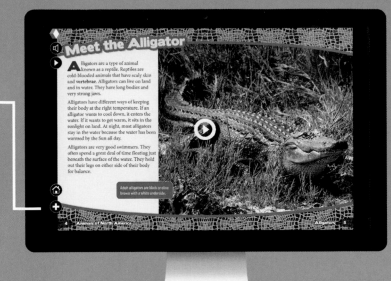

Click on the plus icon ⊕ found in the bottom left corner of each spread to open additional teacher resources.

- Download and print the book's quizzes and activities
- Access curriculum correlations
- Explore additional web applications that enhance the Lightbox experience

LIGHTBOX DIGITAL TITLES
Packed full of integrated media

VIDEOS
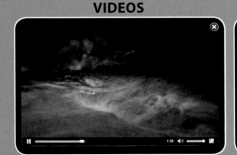

INTERACTIVE MAPS
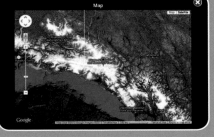

WEBLINKS

SLIDESHOWS

QUIZZES

OPTIMIZED FOR
✓ **TABLETS**
✓ **WHITEBOARDS**
✓ **COMPUTERS**
✓ **AND MUCH MORE!**

Published by Smartbook Media Inc.
350 5th Avenue, 59th Floor New York, NY 10118
Website: www.openlightbox.com

Library of Congress Control Number: 2015942496

ISBN 978-1-5105-0098-3 (hardcover)
ISBN 978-1-5105-0099-0 (multi-user eBook)

Editor: Katie Gillespie
Designer: Mandy Christiansen

Printed in the United States of America in Brainerd, Minnesota
1 2 3 4 5 6 7 8 9 0 19 18 17 16 15

062015
030615

Every reasonable effort has been made to trace ownership and to obtain permission to reprint copyright material. The publisher would be pleased to have any errors or omissions brought to its attention so that they may be corrected in subsequent printings. The publisher acknowledges Getty Images and iStock as its primary image suppliers for this title.